100 Words in 30 Nights

Sensual Thoughts in Life's Seasons

T.L. Rawlings

Published by

THE HARRISON GROUP

Copyright 2014 by T.L. Rawlings. All rights reserved.

All rights reserved. No part of this book may be used or reproduced in any manner whatsoever without written permission except in the case of brief quotations embodied in critical articles and reviews.

Interior design by Jessica Tilles for TWA Solutions

Printed in the United States of America

ISBN 13: 978-0-9669772-5-4

DEDICATION

I dedicate this book to every
muse of my life's journey.

Good, bad, and beautifully ugly.

To Rah, thank you for being in existence.
From you I've found, and we've birthed, the
greatest gifts of LIFE (Zoe), which are
LOVE unconditional, and JOY unspeakable.
I love you, and if we just believe,
the best is yet to come!

ALSO BY T.L. RAWLINGS

But...Naked Honest?

TABLE OF CONTENTS

Autumn

Forgive Him	11
Should I	16
Lace	20
Drip	22
Candy	24
ATP	27
The Bewitching Hour	31
Not Bad Meaning Bad	35
Sex Appeal	38

Winter

Ready	43
Joella	45
Cheeks	49
Vegas Nights	51
An Angel Appeared	53

Spring

Blue 61
My Spiritual 63
Freedom..69

Summer

Wordsmith 73
Busy Body..76
HOLLYWOOD Child 78
Now..81

Message from T.L. Rawlings 85
Thank You..87

100 Words in 30 Nights

Sensual Thoughts in Life's Seasons

AUTUMN

Forgive Him

※

I usually don't speak on another's behalf

but...please

forgive him...

for creating you in such beauty and fulfillment that one day your being created second would cause him to second guess you

forgive him...

for only being man enough not to take the lead until after the mistake was made

forgive him...

for accusing you of his downfall

forgive him...

for treating you less than perfect

forgive him...

for holding you down during sex, but not holding your hand through the birth

forgive him...

for committing to pursuit, but not forever

forgive him...

for walking away from you barefooted, but complaining as you try to fill his shoes

forgive him...

for leaving you unprotected as he searched for new land

forgive him...

for turning a deaf ear to your cry

forgive him...

for getting frustrated when you sigh

forgive him...

for getting pissed when you vent

forgive him...

for not realizing you were sent...to him

forgive him...

for blaming you for being you

forgive him...

for flowing in your moods

forgive him...

for taking on your moons

forgive him...

for trying on your shoes

forgive him...

for not playing his position

forgive him...

for wanting you to cook, but not providing food nor kitchen

forgive him...

for wanting sex now

forgive him...

because that romantic stroll will have to wait a while

forgive him...

for being his father's child

forgive him...

because he watched depression hide behind a smile

forgive him...

for not knowing what to say

forgive him...

for spitting out immediate words anyway

forgive him...

for his silence

forgive him...

for trying to avoid the violence...in him

forgive him...

for treating you like a girl

100 Words in 30 Nights

forgive him...

for not treating you like a girl

forgive him...

again and again...and again

forgive him...

forgive me...

forgive...

for...give

Should I

let him know that

i want him

that

i don't believe in restraint

the shit i think about

could make the average guy faint

of heart

see

i play for keeps

under and behind sheets

i

turn myself out

because

well let's face it

100 Words in 30 Nights

all i need is

what i like

right?

i need what

i

like right now

if it's tasty

to me it's tasteful

mine just for that time

because who needs the fucking

drama

save it for yours

not this mama

i like

what

i like

when i

like it

i

want it

when i

want it

and he knows

that's why when he calls

i nod

he drives over

and he gives it to me

the way

i like

it

how

i

like it

so why

100 Words in 30 Nights

should i

ever

wait

should i?

Lace

there's something

there's something she's not telling me

I know her

that smirk

it says

I have a secret

she says

I know something

something you don't know

but

will please you

something to exalt you

not just meant to

100 Words in 30 Nights

tease you

delicate

erotic

unnoticeable to

surface eyes

only my

Superman

will recognize

that which lies

deeper

can't wait

to see your face

later

when you see

my lace...

Drip...

wouldn't it be nice

just, wet

I mean, that moisture your cat gets...that liquid situation

that you could never regret

that

flow of emotions from your natural pet

that juice that makes your makeup a wreck

that sweat that makes your do a mess

that

electric blue

that

100 Words in 30 Nights

voodoo

that ooooooooohhhhhuuuuuuhhhooooooo

if it's all in your mind

that's

fine

because i will act in every scene

whether awake...or just a

wet

dream

Candy

I have thing for chocolate

but

only when i want it

see

i'm not a candy-holic

but

i...i...

love the taste

of

the sweet essence

nostalgic adolescence

i get

giddy

100 Words in 30 Nights

in its presence

i mean

i can go for weeks...

without getting weak

but when i do

it's that chocolate with nuts i seek

that whatchamacallit, peppermint patty, that reeses pieces, milky way even sugar daddies...

but every now and then I

i flip

on the caramel tip

dripping in my mouth, taste buds going crazy

all inside and no one knows

i'm feigning...an addict for it

that good ol'

chocolate

it calls me...

not good for me in excess...

but as long as i have access

I will indulge...with an ever-glooming fear...of...

the bulge

ATP

(Assume the Position)

❧

the all-points-bulletin went out

"be on the lookout...armed and dangerous"

he couldn't believe it had come to this

it had all went too far

and now

someone had to pay

someone had to go down

the crimes were undeniable

though committed in passion

the evidence convicted her

as her location was revealed

they surrounded the building

they sent their best man in

they knew he would find her

corner her and

take her down

though the building was extremely well lit

he couldn't find her

his heart began to race

as he climbed the stairs

he could smell her perfume

as he turned the corner he could hear her breathing

"up against the wall!"

he commanded

she turned to the wall

and assumed the position

he checked her thoroughly

then turned, closed and locked the door

he started from her head

and worked his way down

he could no longer

contain his urge...he could feel her pulse as he caressed her curves

his hunger

which had passed down from centuries before

had to be tamed

and she

was of the same kind

as she spread her legs

with her hands against the wall

he whispered in her ear "It's time"

as she moaned

he grabbed her hair to expose her toned neck

as tears slid down his face

his fangs began to pierce through his gums

his senses were exploding, hearing every sound every creature of the night

yet they were in the light

TL Rawlings

nothing hidden

as he thrust his teeth into her luscious flesh she grabbed his head

with her beast coming forth

she clawed the wall until the paint began to rip

he ripped away her dress and

slid his throbbing sword into her hot pussy

as he thrust, she pushed off the wall causing erotic vibrations heard for miles

he scratched her back until the blood and sweat ran together

as she turned around she pushed him against the wall

the lioness climbed him like a tree

and wrapped her powerful legs around him riding his dick in midair

as he began to explode inside her she whispered in his ear...

"now you die, for a moment"

the creatures were unleashed into the night

The Bewitching Hour

charm

that fascination

see

it comes about 1am

maybe 3

when you feel those erotic eruptions

you can't see

where

your mind invites

your body to explore your

sexuality

that time where your body is endless

all senses tingle

nerves erect

and sweating

that murderous hour

where asphalt turns into demons

where victims die

and crimes rise

that hour where the flesh thrives

behind closed doors

bodies roar

images mesh together

in forms of majestic ecstasy

no need for names

for the spirits are the same

more than a fuck game

2 beings on the same page

we are here

to handle business

it's fucking serious

no need for conversation

beyond masturbation

100 Words in 30 Nights

what old folks call relations

we call releasing frustration

stress relief

redirecting grief

for a moment

we forget

we don't even love each other

because making love

was never the plan

just blowing out backs till neither one of us could stand

that time where the sun sleeps

that time where married individuals creep

that time where wolves devour sheep

that time where beds don't squeak

see

the floor is where we are

fucking hard

becoming a part of our environment

this can't be heaven sent...nah

feels too fucking good

almost like

love should

Not Bad Meaning Bad

I mean

that's just the way she is.

She does those things that

pride never finds easy

to forgive.

She

excavates hearts of all

reasons to live,

without her.

TL Rawlings

She makes the grass on the other side seem

brown.

She specializes in turning smiles upside down.

She lives out daydreams

in night scenes like a dope fiend nodding but still contemplating her next scheme.

She's sexy deadly, yet

easy heavy...

you get me?

She's that weight on your shoulders, yet

the strength to move boulders...

you get me?

She's the cool on your neck, yet

the burn in your chest.

100 Words in 30 Nights

She's the calm in your sleep, yet

the stroke in your freak.

She's the smile in your sigh, yet

the reason doves cry.

And worst of all...

she has no clue,

what her presence or

absence can do.

See she's bad.

Wait.

Not bad meaning bad,

but bad meaning...

Damn.

SEX APPEAL

you know

that thing that separates

you from me

you know

you being she

me being he

it's a sex thing

we think differently

because we

be differently

raised we were

you with dolls

me with balls

you nurturing

100 Words in 30 Nights

me playing

you nurturing

me playing

while I went from

balls to trucks

play to work

you escalated to

barbie

creatively dressing and expressing every

grown and sexy attitude through plastic

which embodied a world of emotions

and when homegirl was ready to explode

there came ken

relationship stories by 7

while my emotions were wrapped up

in game

tears from my eyes were only justified

from losing

competition kept us on edge

trophies our goal

winning our standard

game

perfecting game by 15

fast girls want love

fast boys want to win

get it

we think differently

that's all

you learned through emotion

i learn through trial and error

sex

our differences

appeal

draw us together

WINTER

Ready

it's that point when a 14inch dick can't touch that spot

feel me

cumming 6 times...in one night isn't enough

you're never ready when it comes

but you never want it to end

it's never hurt so good

or felt so bad

you shiver in the heat and sweat in the cold

it's the only place where perfection is found

the only place where there is no ground

it's the destination

and the ride

it's the place where

feelings can't hide

the place where noun meets verb

where you have to act out this word

the place where ugly

is beautiful

funk is perfume

where ...

where...

fuck it...

love

JOELLA

I gave you my word

my promise

that I would never leave you

my word

my promise

that i would fill every void

my word

my promise

that every day i'm with you

the sun will rise

my word

my promise

that every breath you take would include me

that i would be the salt of every tear you cry

i will preserve you

the exhale of every sigh

my word

my promise

that if you ask of me

i will

if you ask of me

i will

see

i am always mindful of you

i am

the answer to every why

i am the answer to every sigh

every cry

i am

the completion of every prayer

100 Words in 30 Nights

i am

the reason your feet hit the ground

the reason you hear sound

the reason you feel...

anything

the reason you smell the beauties of Spring

the reason you see the light

the delectable taste of night

and if i provide for the birds of the air

how could I not be mindful of my child so fair

how could i see you in despair

and not care

know that i am always there

always more than willing

to share

all that i have

all that i own

TL Rawlings

with you

ask of me

continuously

never faint

i will uphold you

i'm just building you

in love

so that you

will be willing too,

to...

Cheeks

Deep eyes dance above them

Your tone reflects the glow

off those round bursts of joy

Ever expecting

always anticipating

yet never anxious

Always ready to receive

Yet lovingly giving.

Your essence is light to

those who fall in the midst of doubt

those who dwell in despair

those who fiddle in depression...

Yet you never stop,

you never halt that which lies within

from coming forth

bursts of joy...

easily seen...

visible to all,

Explosions that don't kill

but heal.

Only destroying

sadness

Yes

emanates

continually

through,

those beautiful bursts

of joy

Vegas Nights

We could

Take this chance

a simple roll of the dice

puts our realities on the table

when most would keep poker faces

to hide their flaws

those things they think

no one can handle

those that could break their emotional bank

those

those things that

those things that could

give them their biggest winnings

new beginnings

TL Rawlings

those things that could release soul ties

and

dismantle heart strings

so that the beats would be

harmonious with like instruments

a perfect composition

be it friends or lovers

no longer hindering one another

because of

the fear

see

to win

and win big...

you have to place a bet

grab the dice

and

roll

An Angel Appeared...

Holiday cheer

As we trimmed the tree

The pine smell rose through the house

Lights, ornaments, angel hair

and at the top

there she was...

an ebony colored angel in white

glistening with silver traces

elegant

but on her face not a smile

calm

eyes closed

ever peaceful

almost

as if she was thinking

thinking to the Christmas past

when she could only look at the lights in her night season

hoping that this year's gift would be freedom

from the bondage in her own mind and body

freedom

from the hands of those who invaded her purity

freedom

to be a girl not abused by evil intent

freedom

to know love not

physical and emotional pain

nurturing not perversion

I looked again

Noticing her head bowed a bit

Humbling in grace

As if she was calm

Thinking of the present season

Now matured in the eyes of onlookers and acquaintances

Never though

able to grow fully

mature fully

forgive fully

for she was never allowed to

grow fully

Mature Fully

forgive, or love fully

before...

she even had a chance to know herself

her worth

her value

her destiny

now in her calm...humility is present

though not humiliated...

hmmm

As I looked again I noticed her hands

beautifully together...

in a mode of prayer

For her future season

prayer of guidance

covering

direction

amazingly enough

prayer for her abusers

violators

naysayers

haters

and for her seed

mighty in the earth
impacting the world.
I was brought back to reality
as the latter shook...
I straightened her gown...
and slowly stepped down...
Noticing the lower I went
the higher she became...
as I reached the ground...
she was still on top...
beautifully elegant
making this symbol of giving
a finished product.
Her enemies were now
her footstools
There was none higher than her
on this tree of life

TL Rawlings

And to look on her...

all I saw...

was awesome

beautiful

complete

SPRING

Blue

sweat rolls down

leather dark cheeks

hearts pound to

slow tempo beats

heat raises from cellars of dust

wooo

I feel

different now

can those like me in heart and mind

cause happiness

I'm not there

my hips sway like money motivation

I feel

TL Rawlings

crazy girlish yet school boyish

my eyes sting from smoke and sweat

I feel

woooo

the ghosts of tobacco creates waves we ride

synchronized

we all feel lite

heavy dark

we feel

Blue

My Spiritual

Our first stage was less than stable

Oceanic rapids

carried shows on wooden tables

Our tribal stance

turned to aerobic dance

just to enable

Strength

Yet this pretense

was only to prevent

a decrease in silver spent

by buyers

eager to acquire precious cargo
brought to Jamestown

But

before they hit ground

Many would find their graves at sea

Survivors

not knowing what was to be

Their mental positions

Fixed on

retreat, run, flee

And while artifacts

remained in the Motherland

There were demon distracting rhythms

in the claps

of chained banded hands

In shackled feet

the devil's defeat

was a steady pace of victorious beats

100 Words in 30 Nights

Introduction

to biblical chapters

read

"Servants obey your masters..."

which lead to overwhelming instances

of religious disasters.

I guess you could call them

"Illiterate Imposters"

For this book of racial discord

became the same sword

to bring Africa's diverse people

on one accord

toward

freedom

Call and response chants

liberty dance

in negro spirituals

TL Rawlings

Unity through dreary musicals

became their miracles

from Father

Slave masters wouldn't bother

as long as their movement brought

productivity

what they didn't realize

is that Father was freeing them from

captivity

Like those with Moses

God chose this people

to make noise

Ancestors of poetic girls and boys

gifting bursting

Shining stars

like Zora Neale Hurston's

and Paul Lawrence Dunbar's

100 Words in 30 Nights

Jump back honey

seems funny

but since this rhythmic poetry never stopped

Congratulations

the 1800s became the proud parents

of Hip-Hop

The Africans tribulation

became our nations foundation

for music

Like them

I choose to use it

to escape bondage

yet we pay homage

to Christ

to those that gave their lives as sacrifice

that we might write

the Gospel According to us

TL Rawlings

without fuss

Good news made literal

so either in your seat

or on your feet

Please take heed

to My Spiritual

Freedom

Waking up clear

No worrying about need

Sun or rain

You own the day

Foot to ground

Choices

Options

It all seems so simple

Have you ever been here

Before

When palaces were homes

Before

When

Slaves were Kings

When

Daylight brought newness not pain

When

Nightfall brought peace not sadness

When

You could taste the sweetness

You could smell the fragrance

You could see the beauty

When

The sun didn't hurt

The moon didn't chill

When

SUMMER

Wordsmith

Mysterious queen

what a fool believes

no wise man can argue

if I tell you she was mine

it's only in mind

liberty was hers...free to roam

but she wasn't a distant traveler

her destinations were usually home

to her room

where her walls experienced wondrous tales

of 4 cornered dreams without rooftops

in that room lived masterpieces of
profound thought

which if taught

could change project minds to Manhattan penthouse dreams

as she glanced downward and words rose past her head

those walls bled joy like drips of paint

these words could stop domestic violence

in the minds of the victim before it occurred

depression killer

esteem Lifter

bringer of faith

when i think on her i smile

all the while knowing

that for a time...she was mine...but

only in mind...

see she was friends with liberty...

and my cage had no bars...ever

so my cage could hold her never...

100 Words in 30 Nights

see it could never be...

cause me and liberty...

had a fling... too...

Busy Body

Oh he's a busy body
yeah I know the type
never enough time to
speak
not enough days in the week
never enough tick tock
in the 24 hours we all keep
I know his type
his main excuse
is minute abuse
you see
it keeps him from committing
committing to be there
when

100 Words in 30 Nights

when

you want him

to be there

when

when

you need to see him

like he's so precious

oh

there he is

I bet...

"Hey man!

Oh...yeah, I know...

busy right...I just wanted

to say...I love you..."

and

he actually

stopped

HOLLYWOOD Child

The hills are calling

I thought it was a number of things

until I realized the truth

That truth being

That I was Born for this...

born to make noise that the world can hear

and see

born to entertain the masses so that one day

they would listen to me

born to elevate imaginations

through the characters I portray

born to motivate youth and start ciphers

100 Words in 30 Nights

with the words I say

Not born by a river, but on a hill

makes sense

I was born on a mount called St. Joseph

Born to lead a nation into freedom

born to feed the masses

born to impart joy and laughter

born to live

and love

and one day

die...

but not until I

return to the hills

to make noise that the world can hear

and see...

noise that destroys poverty

noise that sets dope addicts free

noise that calls wealth

noise that deams health

NOISE that will continue for generations

multiplying into destinies fulfilled

because my noise...

amplified in those hills

helped to birth

a million dreams.

Now

They tell me we're in the age of Aquarius

Not sure if I believe them

Facts point to technology growing at a rate faster than our compassion

Yet the sun has never blown out

We have more money than ever before

Yet millions are still poor

We have more births

But less parents

More…well

I could go on about despair

But I won't

For I believe now is the dawning of the age of

Restoration

Now is the time to give love

Now is the time to forgive

Now is the time to hold on

To every promise that first came from God

Now redeem

Now rekindle and set ablaze

The passions within until they consume everything that doesn't look like success

Until they consume every negative word ever uttered about you

Over you

To you

Until they ignite the very engine that will drive you into your destiny

And may your destiny influence a life

To live

And not die

For in the age of restoration

100 Words in 30 Nights

We live

And never die

Our dreams are reality

And our reality far exceeds our wildest dreams

Impossibilities perish

And greatness is the new normal

Love reigns

And victory is ours

Now

Message From T.L. Rawlings

If I said I remembered the first time I heard or wrote a poem I'd be lying. But I do remember the first time I realized my poem touched a girl who I liked. It was in elementary school and I was trying to get a smile. After she read the poem, which was about four lines, I spent all night going over, in nervous excitement, about her response, the look in her eyes…it was the greatest thing ever. It was so much more exhilarating than just a smile. The written word went through her eye gate into her mind. There, in her mind, it exploded into euphoric sensory expressions that only she could interpret it as, and then traveled down to her heart, to beat out in her every pulse. Yep, it was like that and her eyes said it all. Immediately I was hooked on the written word. Not just because of how it made me feel to read great stories and verses, but because of what I now knew it did to others.

So my friends, while I love the spoken words of awesome poets around the globe, I will forever be intimately connected to my first true love, which flows out of my heart and through my fingers to pencils, pens and keyboards. The written word allows you to travel in the voice your mind creates, in the characters with whom you want to interact. Until the next time, enjoy the journey.

God Bless, One Love

THANK YOU

To my best friend and partner, Yonder. Thanks for keeping me motivated into success. One more down, 150 more to go! Thank you to all my family and friends. Thank you, Zoe, for bringing me joy every day, even when you're being mischievous. Daddy loves you, baby. Thank you to all those who support and buy books. We love ya! Thank you, Father, for using me as Your microphone.

www.ingramcontent.com/pod-product-compliance
Lightning Source LLC
LaVergne TN
LVHW051153080426
835508LV00021B/2596